Max Overacts Volume One: Hold On To Your Stubs

ISBN 978-0-9879042-0-1

Follow Caanan (And Max!) at occasionalcomics.com

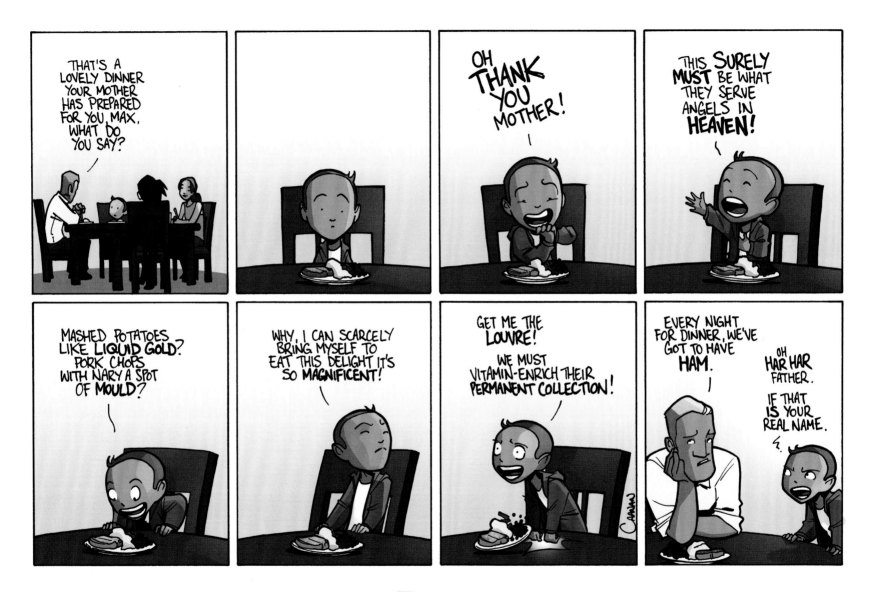

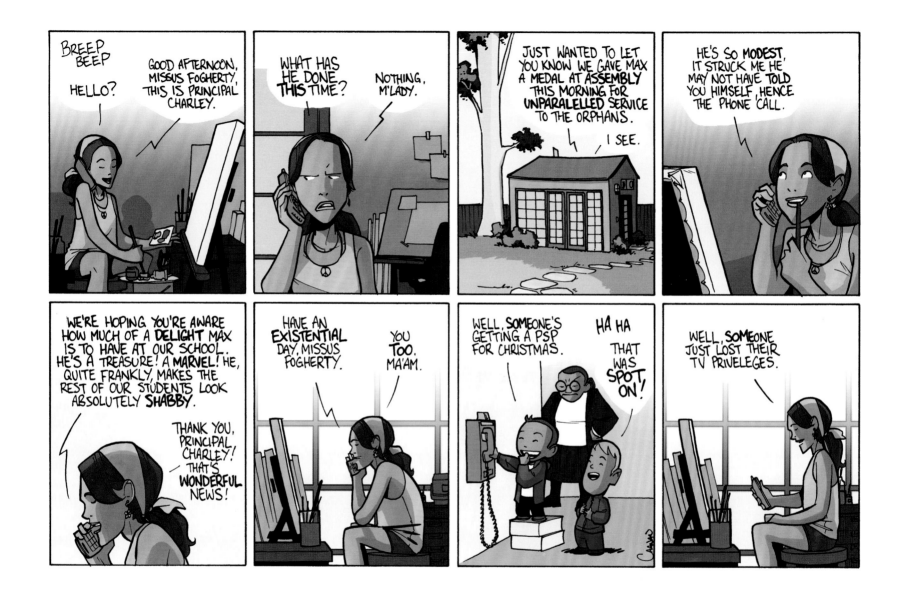

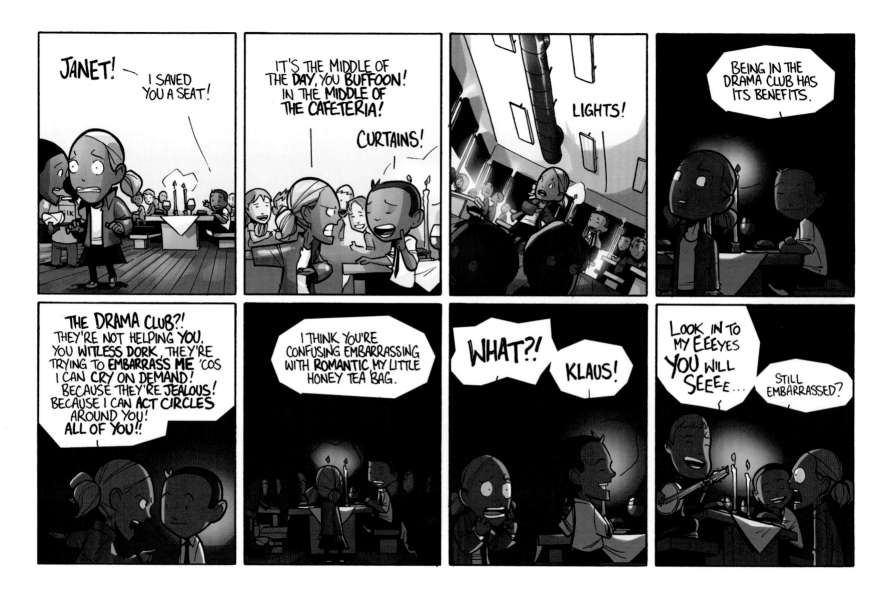

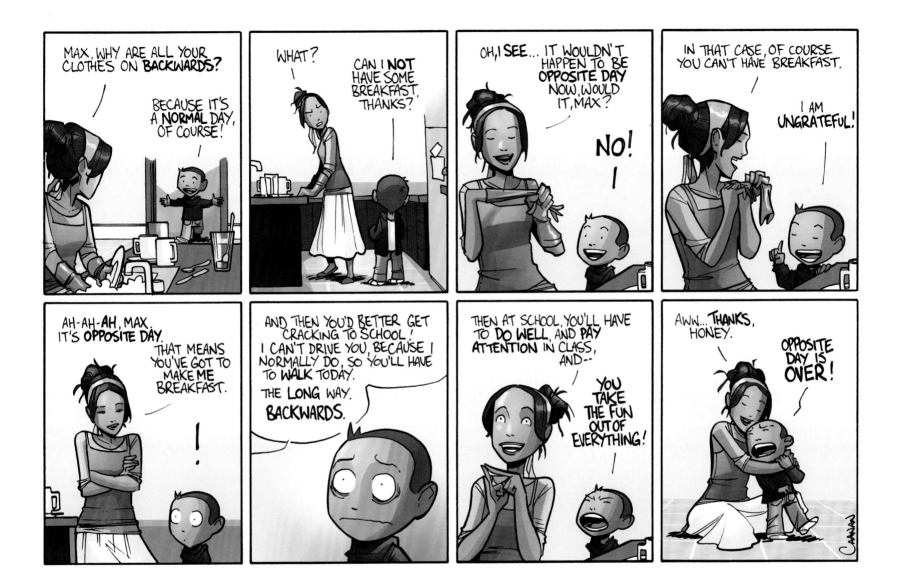

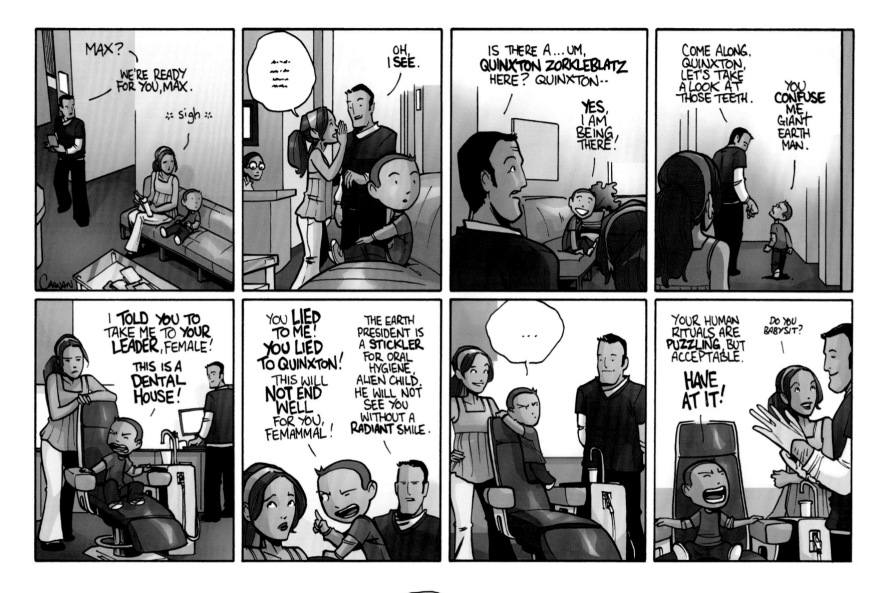

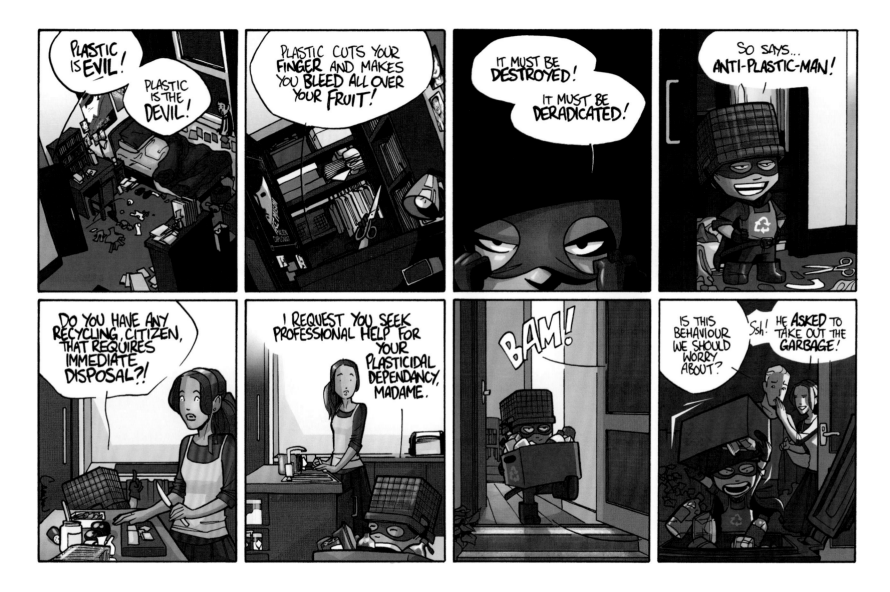

USED CLOTHING IS LIKE WEARING LAYERS OF HISTORY.

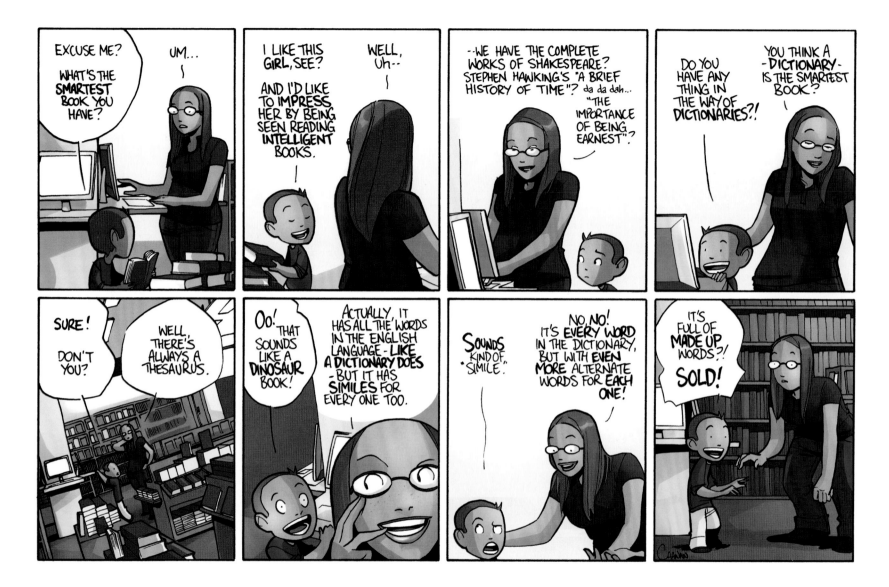

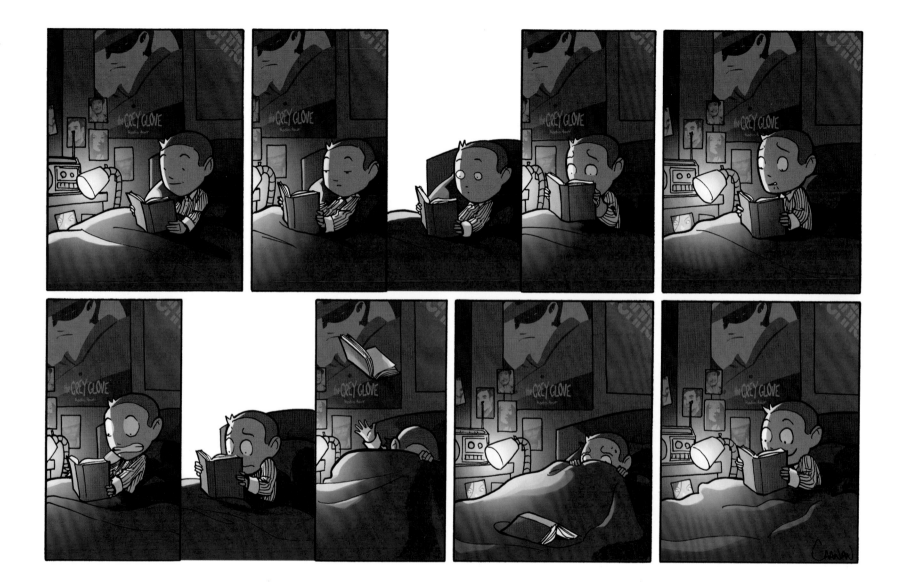

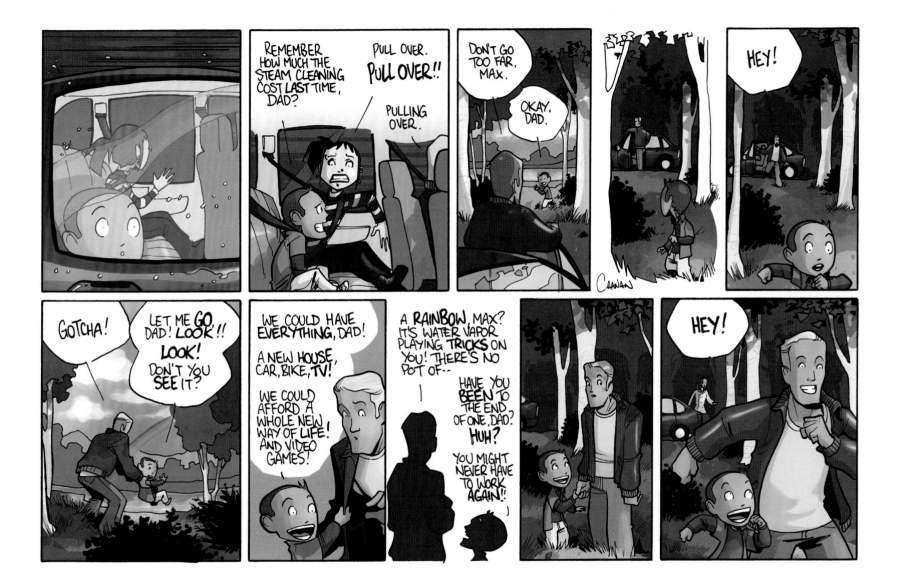

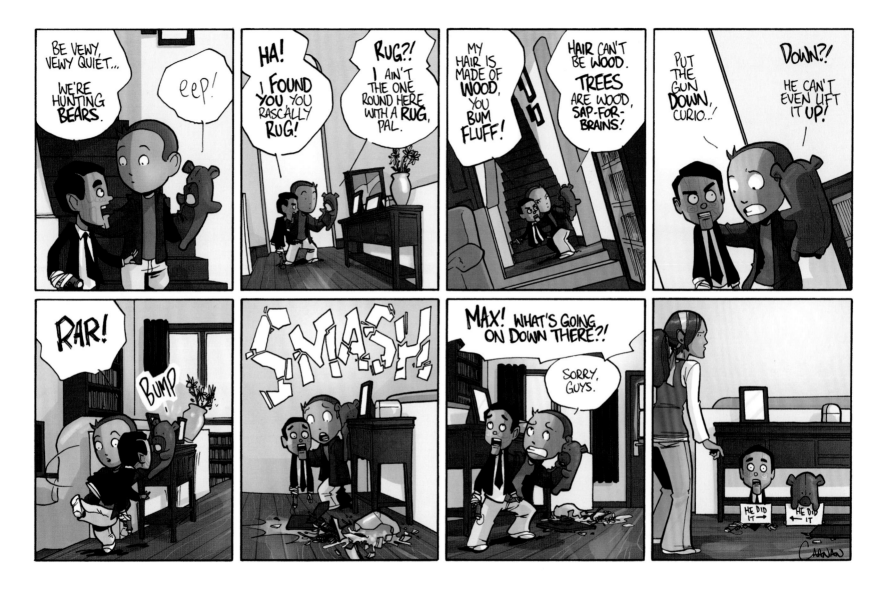

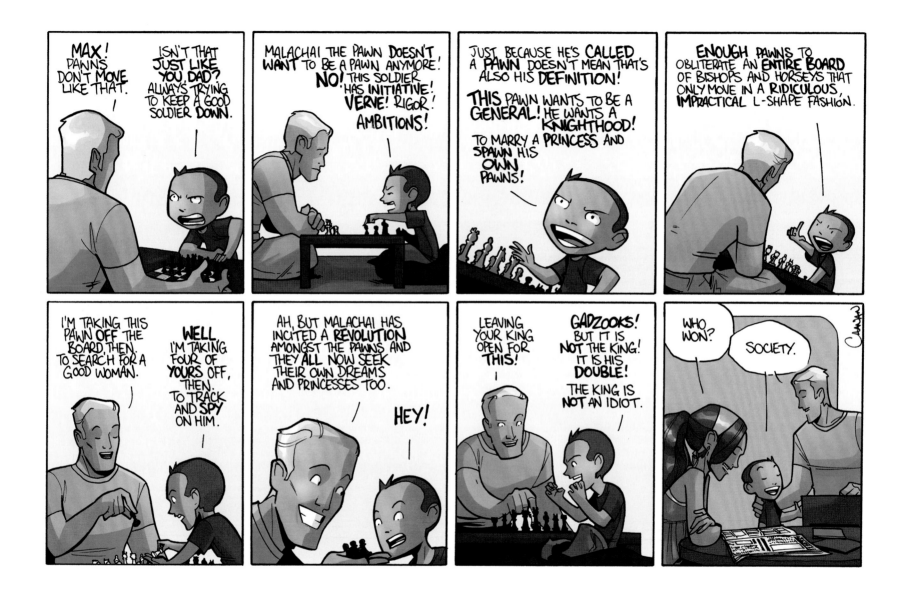

MAKE WAY FOR THE CHAIRMAN OF THE BOARD ...GAME...

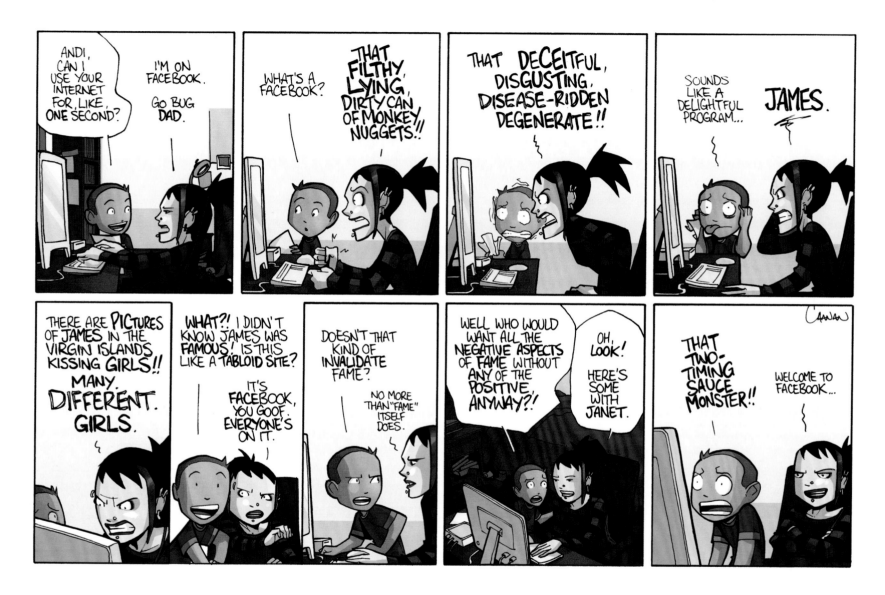

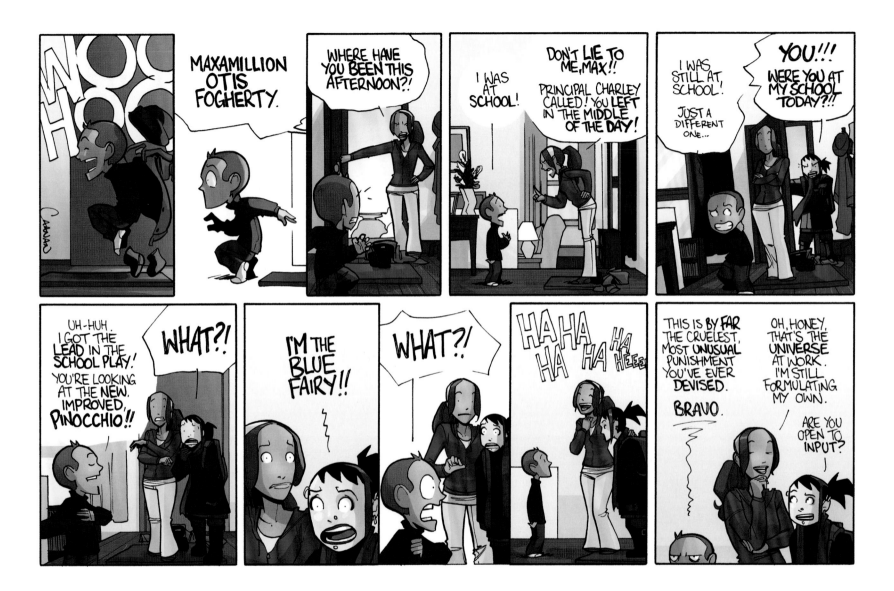

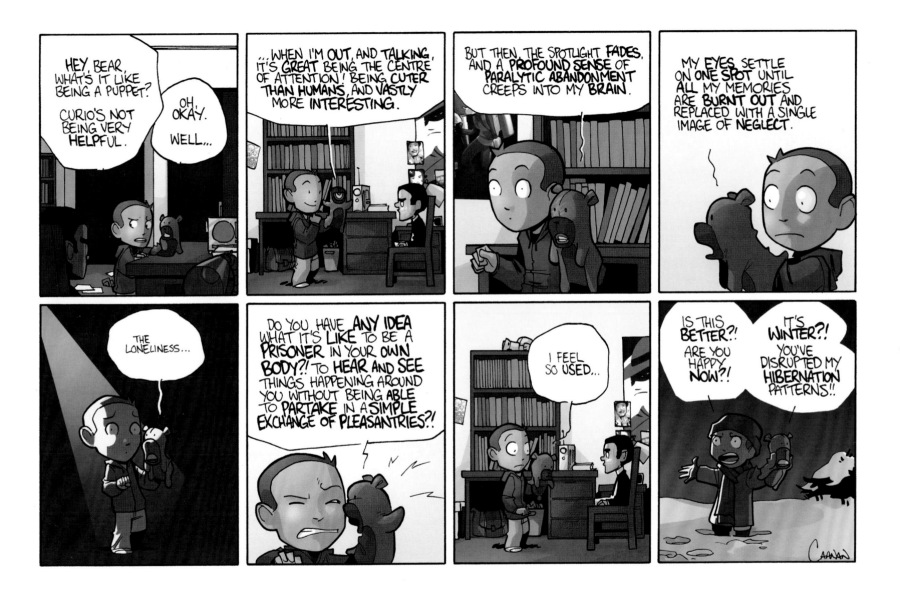

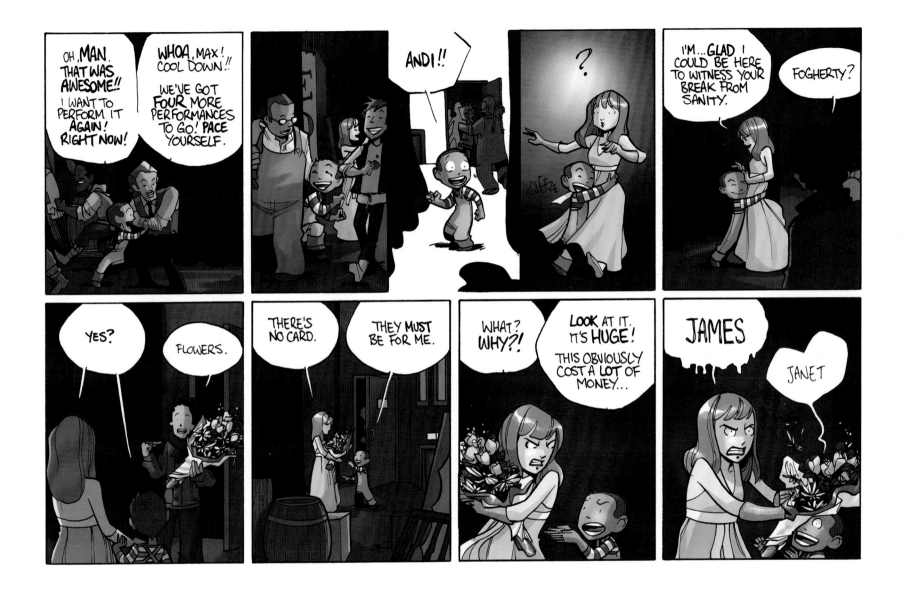

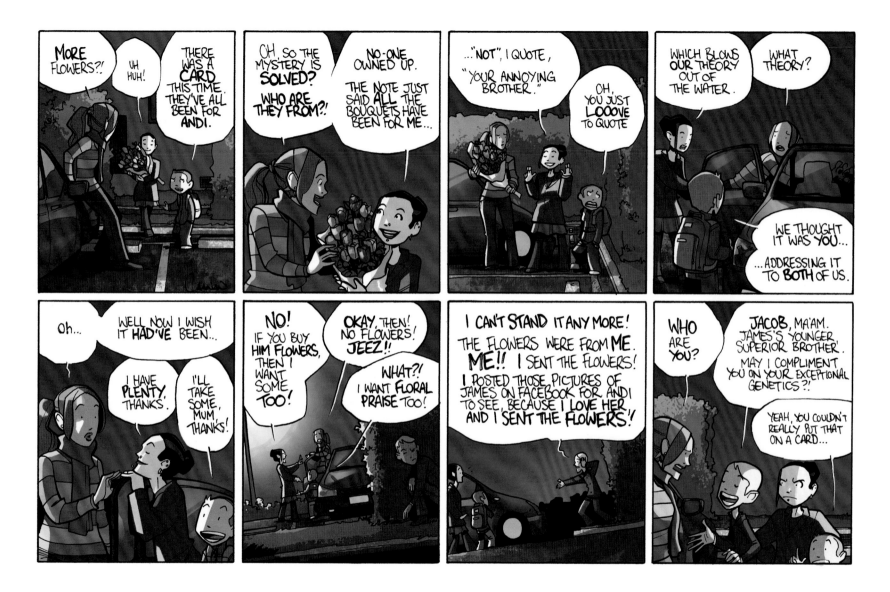

THE RIGHT AUDIENCE OF ONE CAN BEAT THE ENTIRE WORLD STAGE.

IT'S TOUGH TALKING ABOUT THE ELEPHANT IN THE ROOM, WHEN YOU'RE THE ONLY ONE WHO SEES IT.

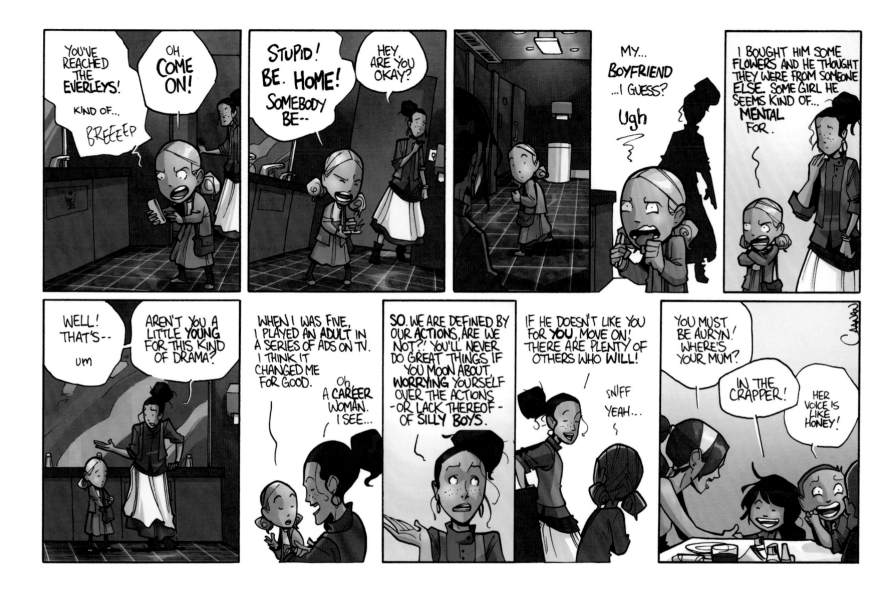

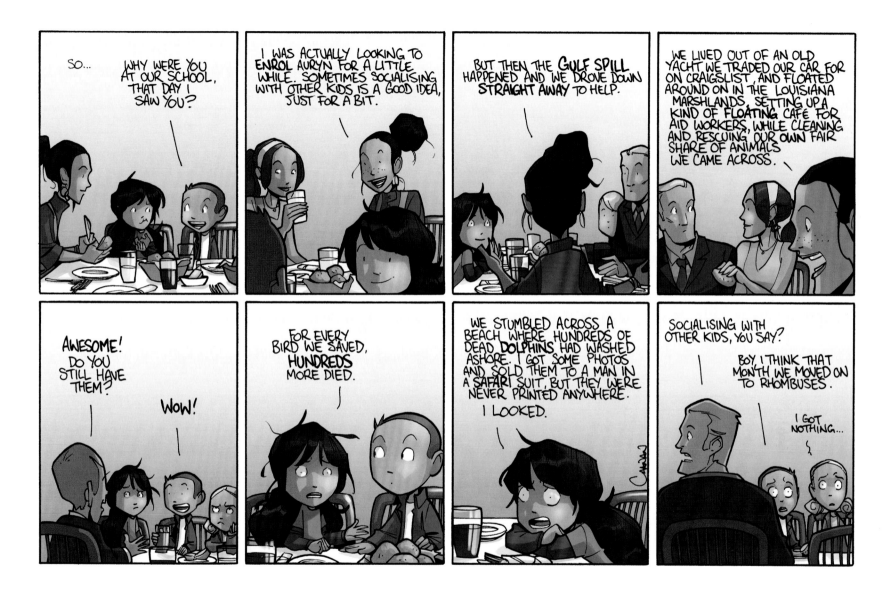

SO... WHY WERE YOU AT OUR SCHOOL, THAT DAY I SAW YOU?

I WAS ACTUALLY LOOKING TO ENROL AURYN FOR A LITTLE WHILE. SOMETIMES SOCIALISING WITH OTHER KIDS IS A GOOD IDEA, JUST FOR A BIT.

BUT THEN THE GULF SPILL HAPPENED AND WE DROVE DOWN STRAIGHT AWAY TO HELP.

WE LIVED OUT OF AN OLD YACHT WE TRADED OUR CAR FOR ON CRAIGSLIST, AND FLOATED AROUND ON IN THE LOUISIANA MARSHLANDS, SETTING UP A KIND OF FLOATING CAFÉ FOR AID WORKERS, WHILE CLEANING AND RESCUING OUR OWN FAIR SHARE OF ANIMALS WE CAME ACROSS.

AWESOME! DO YOU STILL HAVE THEM? WOW!

FOR EVERY BIRD WE SAVED, HUNDREDS MORE DIED.

WE STUMBLED ACROSS A BEACH WHERE HUNDREDS OF DEAD DOLPHINS HAD WASHED ASHORE. I GOT SOME PHOTOS AND SOLD THEM TO A MAN IN A SAFARI SUIT, BUT THEY WERE NEVER PRINTED ANYWHERE. I LOOKED.

SOCIALISING WITH OTHER KIDS, YOU SAY? BOY, I THINK THAT MONTH WE MOVED ON TO RHOMBUSES. I GOT NOTHING...

SCHOOL SHOULD TEACH MORE LIFE LESSONS, LESS MATH LESSONS.

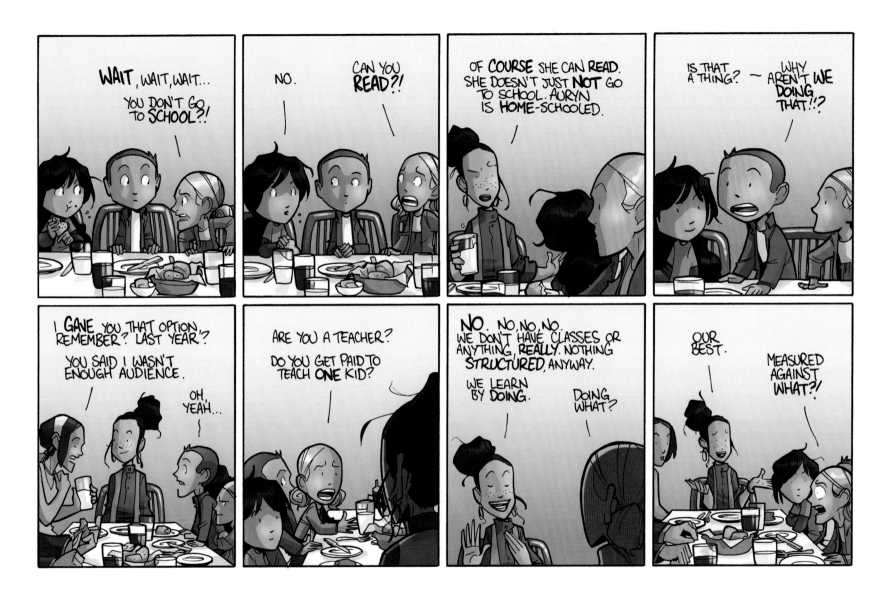

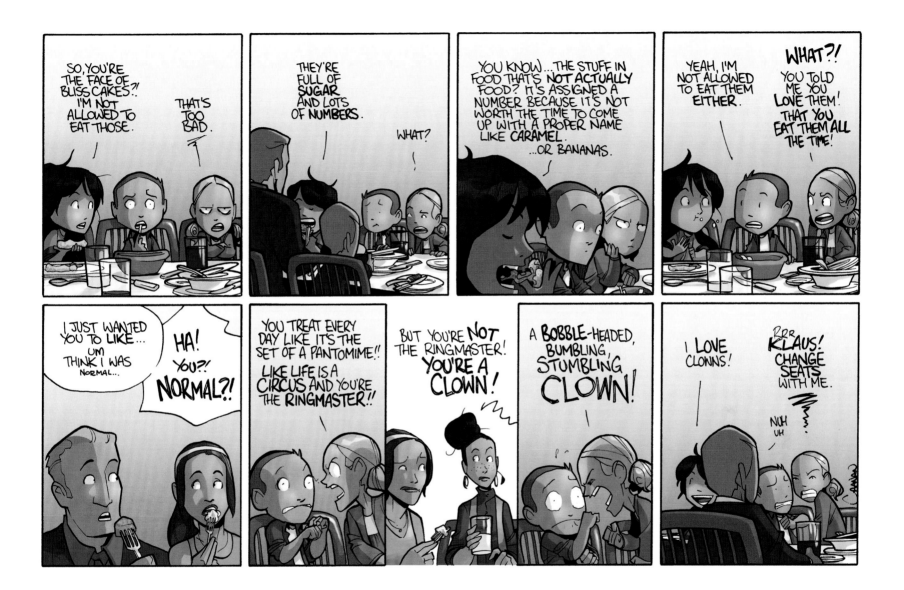

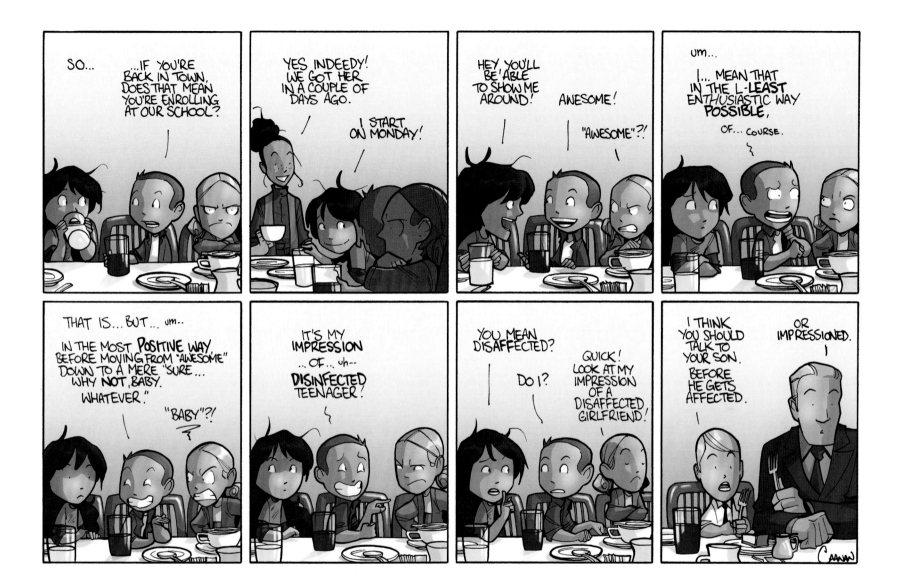

IT'S TOUGH BEING THE NEW KID, 'SPECIALLY IF YOU'RE WEIRD.

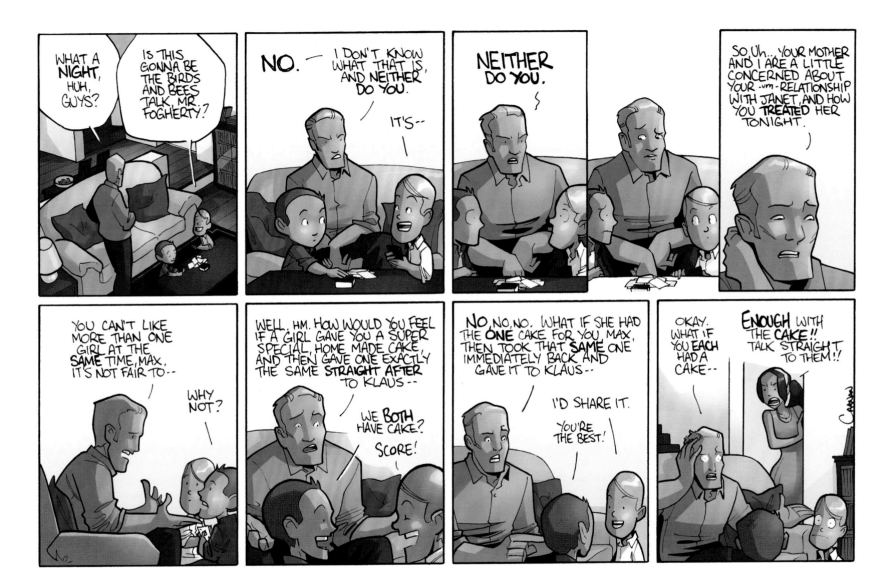

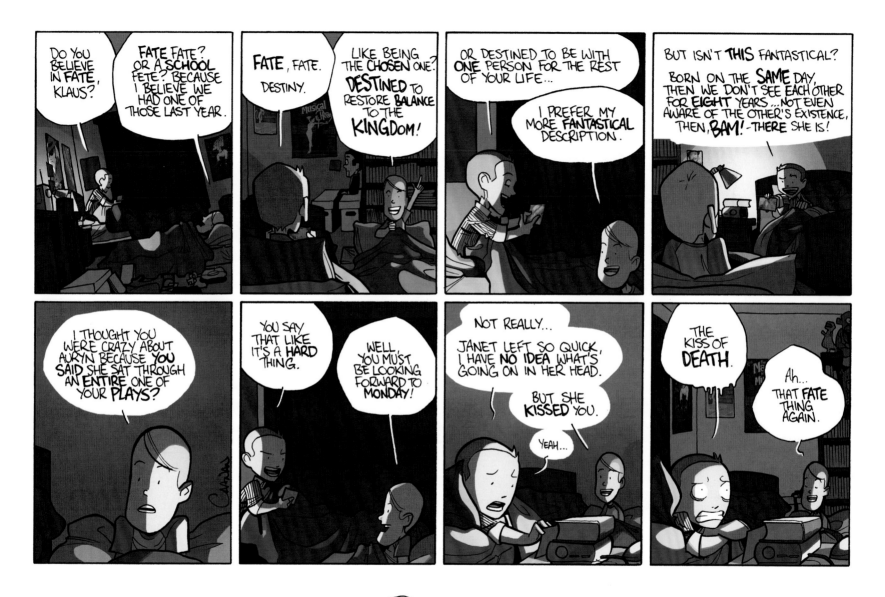

FOLLOW THE ADVENTURES ONLINE
AT OCCASIONALCOMICS.COM